IS GOD REALLY NECESSARY?

A Glimpse Into the Mind of an Atheist

Casey Dorman

Avignon Press
Newport Beach

Cover Picture: Atheist Symbol Created by Diane
Reed. Public Domain

Dorman, Casey, Is God Really Necessary—
religion-philosophy-atheism-spirituality

ISBN: 978-0692224885

Avignon Press
Newport Beach, California, USA

Other Books by Casey Dorman

To My Wife, Lai

Table of Contents

Chapter 1

Why Am I Writing This?

I am an atheist. Being an atheist is not the primary way in which I identify myself, either to others or to myself, but it may be the most misunderstood aspect of who I am. This book is my attempt to explain how atheism fits into my life and how I think about a number of life's issues. Again, it is just my own take on things, and I do not speak for any other atheists. I am not writing this book in response to those who attack atheism. I have been criticized but never really attacked for my beliefs (or you might say, non-beliefs). But many of those whom I admire and with whom I share many opinions, such as those in the peace movement or those in the ecology movement, have written about the role of their spiritual beliefs in their commitments and have even voiced the opinion that without such spiritual beliefs such commitments would be impossible. I would like to show them that they are wrong—not because I want to challenge *their* spiritual beliefs but because I want to erase a barrier they seem to have erected between themselves and someone such as me who lacks such beliefs.

My spiritual friends are prone to say that I may not believe in any religion or in an anthropomorphized god, but since I think that my own life has meaning, and I have an affinity for peace, love, brotherhood, etc., then I am "spiritual" and not a true atheist. I know that saying that makes them feel better, but I am sure that I do not fit any of their definitions of "spiritual." I do not believe in *any* sort of divine power, in *any* sort of existence beyond the physical one or in *any* guiding principle that has its own sense of purpose (e.g. nature's will, the wisdom of the universe, etc.). I do not believe that some "force" which somehow was imbued with a purpose was required to start the universe, nor that any force other than physical ones keeps it going. I am a materialist through and through, not in the sense of valuing material possessions above all else, but in the sense of believing that the material universe is all that exists. I will get into this more later, but first let me tell you how I arrived at my present stage of belief.

Is God Really Necessary?

Chapter 2

Atheism Can Be A Journey

My pathway to atheism was hardly a straight one. I did not grow up in a family which embraced atheism. The religious sentiments of my parents were always obscure to me. When I was a child, my parents never attended any church, although they dutifully dropped me and my brother and sister off at Sunday School. When we were young, around five to ten years old, I seem to remember going to Sunday School just about every Sunday, but when we reached early adolescence the decision became each of our own and my attendance, as well as that of my siblings became spotty. My grandparents (at least on my mother's side of the family) attended the Christian Science church and my grandmother's occupation was as a Christian Science "Practitioner." She actually conducted her "practice" in an office in the same building as my dentist (her services were a lot less painful).

Christian Science is an unusual religion. It was founded by a woman, Mary Baker Eddy, in the late 19th century in Massachusetts. The core beliefs, as I understand them, are that god created everything, including humans, which he created in his own image. The deduction from this premise is that if god is perfect, then whatever he created in his own image must also be perfect, ergo: humans are perfect. Humans, however are subject to "errors" in their thinking, which cause them not to see their own perfection (a curious flaw in their perfection, but one required in order to explain an apparently imperfect world). That is why they get sick and die. That is even why they exist in physical form, which is essentially an illusion, since the essence of being a perfect human is to exist only in spirit. In this scenario, at least as I understood it when I learned it at a young age, Jesus' life was a demonstration that humans are perfect and that death is an illusion—Jesus being a human whose understanding about his relationship to god was more advanced than most other humans'. Jesus was an example for the rest of us to emulate. God, in this system, is the *idea* of perfection and is immaterial (material things being by their nature, imperfect) rather than an anthropomorphized person in heaven (why would god exist as a copy of our material form if that form is a product of an error in our thinking and why would he be located in some material place?). Rather than being a place, heaven is the state of knowing the truth about all of these things.

Mary Baker Eddy took her view of things, she said, from the Bible, and her main teachings were in a book (*Science and Health*), which purportedly explained the Bible. Most of her book's passages were keyed to Bible passages. The most well-known feature of Christian Science is its aversion to medicine. Since illness results from errors in one's thinking and the essence of being human is spiritual, not material, to use doctors or medicine to cure an illness is to give in to materialistic thinking. Instead, good Christian

Is God Really Necessary?

Scientists read the Bible or *Science and Health* in order to correct their thinking. If they need additional help, they go to "practitioners" such as my grandmother. Practitioners do not pray for people in order to induce god to intercede and cure them, rather they actively try to explain the "truth" to their clients in order to change their thinking.

My parents took me to the Christian Science Sunday school, probably more to please my grandmother than anything else, but they also encouraged me and my siblings to attend other churches in town so we could make up our own minds. They also regularly took me to the doctor for checkups or when I was ill. My grandmother would visit me when I was sick, but I never had the sense that my parents gave any credence to her efforts as a serious way to combat illness. (I always pleaded with my parents, that, as a Christian Scientist, I should be excused from the requirement that all school children be vaccinated against various diseases—since I detested needles. Thankfully, my parents never gave in to my pleas.)

Clearly, my religious education was outside of the mainstream and included mixed messages regarding how seriously I should take religion. My own religious ideas and commitments vacillated over the years, well into my adulthood. For a period of about a year in high school I attended the Christian Science church more or less regularly with my girl friend. She was not a Christian Scientist herself, but my parents disliked me seeing her and my grandmother was more accepting of her, and I think that I felt an obligation to give something back to my grandmother by my church attendance. When I went off to college, I at first attended a few meetings of campus Christian Scientists, but they were so much more committed to the intricacies of the religion than I was that I did not feel as though I had found any kindred spirits and I stopped attending their meetings. In my sophomore year, like many young people, I was completely swayed by philosophical arguments against the existence of god and became, for a short while, an atheist. But I could not quiet my inner voice, which, probably out of habit, begged for forgiveness each time I did something wrong and asked for help whenever I found myself in trouble. My atheism soon waned. I was not convinced of the truth of any particular religion and I thought of myself as an agnostic—there was someone or something listening to my pleas but I had no real idea whom or what it was.

Following college (which for me went on for ten years, since I stayed on to earn a Ph.D.), I stayed pretty much agnostic, but took up reading the Bible. I focused almost exclusively on the early chapters of the New Testament, because I found Jesus' message inspiring (Paul, on the other hand, sounded to me as if he was a vengeful, paranoid zealot). Probably because of the influence of my Christian Science upbringing, I was not sure if I regarded Jesus as anything more than a gifted, committed human being, but his example was one that I felt could provide a moral compass for my life. Unfortunately, it was during this period that I also made some of the most serious moral errors of my life, the main one being getting divorced and moving too far away from my children to allow me to be around them regularly. I suffered extreme guilt because of my behavior, not in terms of any fear of punishment or need of forgiveness from god, but because of the harm I knew that I was doing to my children. However, my own immediate, selfish needs (I had fallen in love with someone other than my wife), were a stronger determinant of my behavior than my guilt.

Eventually, after finding a way to reunite with my children and to provide a stronger presence in their lives, I began to drift away from religion. I did not drift in a straight line. I prayed for my children's happiness (not for my forgiveness, because asking for that always seemed too narcissistic to be worthy of prayer and seemed to me to be beside the point, anyway) as well as that of others whom I loved, and I vowed to try to meet whatever need they had, even if doing so compromised my own well-being, partly out of a religiously-based faith that doing the right thing would work out in the end. I didn't always live up to this vow, but I tried.

At some point, probably in my early forties, I began to see my internal religious feelings as a variety of magical thinking. I viewed them as something that was going on inside my head, but with no external referent in the form of a god who was listening to

7

those thoughts. I don't recall any major events that brought on this realization, but I think it was more of a dawning on me that my pleas, promises and whatnots to god were similar to other sorts of magical thinking in which I sometimes engaged. This type of thinking involved minor good-luck rituals (e.g. always tell my wife to drive safely when she left the house or maybe she would have an accident), or efforts to remove negative thoughts from my head by focusing on substitute positive thoughts, etc. It had become clear to me that my pleas to god were a variety of the same thought mechanisms as these good luck rituals and had no more reality to them than had the rituals. (I was never excessively preoccupied with such rituals the way some obsessive neurotics are and I think that my own tendency toward magical thinking was probably typical of most people.)

At the same time that I was re-assessing the function of my dialogues with god (actually monologues, since I had never received any answers back), I was becoming more aware of the fairly ridiculous lengths to which religious people in America seemed to be going to discredit evolution (which I believed in), homosexuality (which I thought was mostly biologically determined and perfectly OK by me) and to promote both militarism and patriotism (did they think that god really favored America and that being Christian meant killing enemies of our country?). I also was aware of the march of science, in physics and cosmology (big-bang theory), chemistry (the Miller-Urey experiments on creating life), biology (cloning and genetics), which began to look to me as if science might have the possibility of explaining enough of the workings of the universe that there would be nothing left for god to explain.

As my appreciation of the explanatory power of science, as well as the validity of its methods grew, my distaste for the simple-mindedness, wishful thinking, and authoritarian methods which characterized religious rebuttals to scientific thinking also grew. Even further, my own research and reading in cognitive psychology, in neuroscience and in philosophy, as well as new developments in evolutionary psychology, led me to believe that even what spiritualists regarded as irreducibly spiritual components of being human could be explained on a material basis.

I emerged from this many-years-long progression in my thinking as a confirmed atheist. I regarded myself as neither religious nor spiritual. I have continued to think this way for at least the last quarter century (I am now in my early seventies). Being aware of my own erratic course toward this destination, I can hardly find fault with others who are somewhere else in their journey or have arrived at a different endpoint in their thinking. But my own atheism has not wavered for many years and, if anything, grows stronger as I get older.

Is God Really Necessary?

Chapter 3

Materialism

I am an atheist because I believe in the material universe (matter and energy) and the laws of the material universe (many of which I don't actually understand, but many of which I do, many of which have not been discovered or for which our current versions are inaccurate, and many of which are purely mathematical and well beyond me and beyond translation into words). To those who argue that there are other things in the world beyond the material (e.g. ideas, meanings, creativity, complexity, etc.), I am not so sure. One interpretation of these variables is that they are non-material emergent properties of interactions at lower level networks of physical components of systems. These new, holistic properties may not be reduced to the properties of the individual components of the interactions. But such emergent properties are just that; they are properties which are still dependent upon the material substrate (e.g. neural interactions, atomic and sub-atomic level activity) without which they would not exist. Another interpretation, however, is that some of these properties, such as meanings, are themselves the way in which animal brains represent their worlds. In this scenario (represented by the work of neuroscientist Walter J. Freeman, for instance), meaning consists of activity patterns in the brain. The interaction of brain states supporting these meanings is the basis of consciousness. The upshot is that, in either interpretation, that of emergent properties or that in which meanings and consciousness are a basic method of representation in the brain, it is the physical properties of the brain which produce meaning and consciousness. (For a fuller discussion of this topic see Appendix B.)

Now some properties of the world, such as honesty, nobility, goodness, evil, etc., all of which are ways in which we characterize people, behaviors, and events in the world, are difficult to imagine as physical properties of the world. Yet some also find them difficult to dismiss as merely subjective judgments. Some people might argue that such qualities represent a non-physical, *higher* kind of property of objects and events. But the truth is, these are simply meanings, on a par with *appetizing,* or *beautiful*, perhaps more heavily dependent upon language than some other meanings, but meanings, nevertheless. As such, they are physical properties of our brains, rather than immaterial properties of the world outside of ourselves, because meanings exist in the organisms who perceive the world, not in the objects they perceive.

In my opinion, all organisms are complex material entities which function according to natural laws, much in the same way that machines do. This includes the thoughts and feelings that human beings have, which also obey natural laws and are produced from complex material processes within human bodies. Human consciousness, in my opinion is the feeling one has when his neurons are processing information via the networks that are in the parts of the brain that processes information consciously. (For an extended discussion of this point of view, see Appendix B.)

But isn't a reliance on only what can be explained by science a limiting point of view? People often say that science has not explained everything, so there is still room for the unknown, the mystical or the spiritual, as forces that affect the working of the universe. In one sense this is true and in another it is not. I find it difficult to conceive of a time at which humans will know the answer to all questions about nature and the universe. Certainly we are not at that time right now. However, we know much more than we did say, 500 year ago. There would have been a lot a "scientist" of 500 years ago could not explain (accurately) about the universe. Many of those things, which were explained by folktales, myth, religion, etc. at that time, now have better explanations because of the advance of science. I have no reason to believe that the same situation will not apply 500 years from now. Much of what we currently can't explain will be explained via science. However, it is true that if we do not have explanations now, that means we cannot rule out some hypotheses and some of these may be spiritual or mystical or religious. If such hypotheses rest upon assumptions that violate what we do know about how nature works however, then I believe it is fair to rule such hypotheses out right now. For instance, if one of our hypotheses requires that the earth and all the life in it was created in seven days and that those seven days were less than 10,000 years ago, then I believe we could rule such an hypothesis out because we have definitive evidence that the earth was not created in seven days or less than 10,000 years ago.

Possibilities that do not violate the laws or findings of science, so far as we know them, but are not presently known to exist, could still exist beyond our present knowledge or in the future. And it is perfectly possible that, since our knowledge of the laws that govern the material universe may be wrong or imperfectly known at this time, new discoveries may open up possibilities that we thought had been ruled out. I don't know what they could be, however even admitting such a possibility still does not give me carte-blanche to *believe* in speculations that have absolutely no scientific evidence for them at this time. I may not be able to rule them out, but being certain of their truth is entirely a different matter.

Science is ultimately a social activity. What is "proven" by science is a matter of consensus by the current scientific community. That does not mean that it is either arbitrary or that it is, as claimed by post-modernists, simply a reflection of our agreed upon prejudices and biases. However, it is impossible for us to remove ourselves from our current social matrix and see where we may be using flawed scientific methods or agreeing on things without considering information we either currently don't

have or don't know is relevant. To give a simple
example, if we had been scientists or scholars around
2500 years ago, it would have been an assumption at
the foundation of our science that the sun revolved
around the earth (the first known proposal that the
earth revolved around the sun was made by
Aristarchus of Samos in the 3rd century, BC). We
wouldn't have had the knowledge or the
observational science to suggest to us that we were
wrong. But we were.

A more recent example from my own field of
psychology comes from the "modern learning
theories" of the 1950's and 60's, developed on the
basis of experiments with pigeons and white rats in
cages. Such theories purported to explain all of
human behavior by extending the "laws" of learning
which emerged from these lower animals to humans.
As an undergraduate student I was taught these laws
as "gospel" and the science that created them as
superior to the "mentalistic speculation" of earlier
(and contemporary, competing) psychologists.
Subsequent research, expanded to include the study
of animals in their natural environments instead of in
cages, plus evolutionary theory, computer models,
and studies of the brain, have shown that it is often a
mistake to generalize about behavioral tendencies
across species and settings and most of the so-called
"laws" of learning are applicable, if at all, only in
highly circumscribed situations. At one point cutting
edge physics dealt with matter only down to the
atomic level; now physics deals with fermions and

bosons, the existence of which was not previously known and the present existence of which is based upon a consensus that the experimental procedures which have shown evidence of these particles are valid. In other words, I believe there is some wiggle-room in stating what science knows for sure.

So science does not know everything and may be wrong about what it thinks it knows about some things. But does this leave us unable to rule out anything? Is there nothing that we can say for sure cannot happen or cannot exist? I believe there are some things that can be ruled out. As an example, let me refer to a situation described in one of my favorite science fiction novels, *The Day the Sun Stood Still*. In this novel (actually three novellas, each written by a different author but dealing with exactly the same situation), the sun stands still in the sky (I think for days) and the stories involve describing how the world reacts. Now it is unequivocally impossible for the sun to suddenly stand still in the sky and everything on earth to remain unaffected, as described in this book (despite the Biblical account of such an event in the book of Joshua). The earth would have to stop its rotation for this to happen (interestingly, the earth's rotation is slowing, but it would take eons for it to actually stop and by that time, the effects would probably have killed all living things on earth). Such an effect has been modeled with computers, showing how the oceans would migrate to the two polar regions and reveal a large equatorial land mass that is now covered by water.

Is God Really Necessary?

The world could not suddenly stop spinning and allow everything on earth to continue unaffected. Do we know this for sure? Yes. Couldn't mysterious forces set aside natural laws and allow such an occurrence? Only in our imaginations. This is a situation that it makes no sense to say is "possible." Similarly, there are myriad other events that can be imagined but violate well established laws of nature so that such events can also be declared "impossible." (For a further discussion of this topic see Appendix C.)

There are other events and entities which can be ruled out, not necessarily by science but because they are conceptual contradictions or misunderstandings. Square circles do not exist. A somewhat popular belief among some spiritualists and even some scientists is that consciousness exists prior to reality and in fact, consciousness creates reality. This is a complex question which cannot be dismissed immediately as a conceptual misunderstanding, although I suspect that that is what it is. At any rate, it has no bearing upon atheism, although it is relevant to materialism. The topic is too complicated to go into here and not immediately pertinent, but I have included an extended discussion of this issue in Appendix A, for those who might be interested.

Chapter 4

Emotions and skepticism

What I have said so far may sound too intellectualized for many of you. A common characterization of atheists is that they are overly intellectualized and non-feeling. They have used logic to rule out god and have turned their backs upon their own spiritual feelings, which they dismiss as unreliable emotions. For those of you who think that being an atheist means being divorced from one's own feelings and sense of connection to other humans, let me relate a story about myself.

I fell in love with psychology through a course I took at a community college in my sophomore year of college (having had to drop out of the four year university because I got married and couldn't afford it). When I returned to the university I majored in psychology and was particularly attracted to social psychological research, which at the time was asking what I considered to be relevant questions about human behavior, such as how do we respond to group pressure, or what induces or protects us from conformity (my master's thesis), etc. But I was also drawn to clinical psychology because I felt that I wanted to provide direct help to people. I was torn between my intellectual interests and my sense of duty to others.

17

Is God Really Necessary?

One day I attended a "grand rounds" at the university hospital psychiatry department. The patient, who was presented in person to the audience, was a young boy, maybe 8 or 9 years old. He had a racing heartbeat, which the doctors said could lead to his death. They explained his malady as psychologically based—on fear. They made an analogy to a small bird, which if held in a closed hand, would die because its heart would race out of control (who knows if any of this was true—at that time all sorts of disorders were labeled "psychosomatic" but have later proved to have physical causes). I remember that I was moved by the young boy's plight. The idea that a child could die because of fear, when there was nothing real for him to be afraid of, was emotionally devastating to me. I immediately vowed that I would devote myself to helping children overcome their fears and psychological problems. I switched from social psychology to clinical psychology, specialized in children and ended up with a forty-year career as a clinical child psychologist (I did manage to do quite a bit of research too, in order to satisfy my intellectual side).

I use this example to show the intense and long-lasting effect an emotional experience may sometimes have. What I experienced with the young boy tapped into a side of me that I have been aware of ever since—my sympathy for young people and more generally all people, and my empathy for their distress. This has served me well as a psychologist, but unfortunately made me too indulgent as a parent, grandparent, uncle, and boss. But where did this side of me come from? I have no idea. It's just part of me. But it is a part of me to which I listen, and which may, at times, overrule my reason.

So I am not unemotional. I even allow my emotions to determine many of my decisions. But I am a skeptic. And although I am not unemotional, I am suspicious of information that is accompanied by highly emotional displays. Too much enthusiasm, or anger, or sorrow accompanying an idea raises my antennae. People are easily carried away by their emotions and when they are, they are prone to believe most anything. What makes me even more wary is when a lot of people believe the same thing. So the ideas I am most skeptical about are those that generate a lot of emotion and which are believed by a lot of people. I am most skeptical about those ideas because they are the ideas that are most likely to be unexamined. My skepticism and wariness about emotionally charged ideas probably looks like a lack of emotion to some people, but it is not. It's just skepticism.

Is God Really Necessary?

Chapter 5

The Meaning of Life
(an embarrassingly short chapter)

So I am a materialist through and through. I not only believe that the world around us is composed entirely of material substances (matter and energy) and the laws that govern them, but I believe that human beings are too. I can hear some of you voicing your horror. You are probably saying to yourselves, but isn't a life composed entirely of material things, a life without meaning? Isn't some sense of a higher purpose to life necessary to give life meaning?

Certainly I can have a purpose for my own life. I'm not at all sure what a "higher" purpose than that would be. Does it mean that life itself has a purpose, independent of the thoughts of the people who live those lives? But life itself is an abstract idea, it does not exist separately from individual lives (not necessarily human). Because it does not exist, it cannot have a purpose. But what about a meaning to life? Meanings exist in people's *minds* (from a materialist perspective, in their *brains*), so if a person thinks that life is meaningful, then it has meaning for the person who thinks that. My own life has meaning to me because I care about it, I shape it, I have goals for it and I judge it. My life may have meaning to someone else and his or her life may have meaning to me if we figure in each other's plans, hopes, goals, satisfactions or dissatisfactions. Beyond that, the idea of life having an inherent meaning separate from the human consciousness that thinks about it, has no meaning.

Some people, I know, believe that the purpose and meaning of life are provided by some force or being outside of us (us being the human beings who think about these things). I don't plan to quarrel with their point of view (at least not in this book), but it goes without saying (although I will say it) that since I don't believe in the existence of any force or being with purpose outside of living things, I don't agree that some such outside force or being can provide life a purpose of meaning. That's part of the point of being an atheist.

Chapter 6

Spirit

But, you might say, isn't your material view of humans limited because it does not include the most essential characteristic of humans, which is their spirit. If you mean that humans sometimes persist in the face of almost certain failure, or make great sacrifices for lofty goals, or survive almost impossible circumstances, yes they do and it's fair to label this the human spirit. But this does not signal the presence of something beyond human flesh or human thought that is working by using a power of its own. This is just a convenient, short-hand way of talking about persisting in the face of obstacles, which people do because that is the nature of people (some more than others).

OK, you say, so the human spirit actually refers to some very human characteristics, which are shown by some people in incredibly difficult circumstances, but what about every human possessing a *divine* spirit? Of course my view is that there is no supreme being to contribute a divine spirit, nor is there a source of energy or thought or power other than that which comes from the material world and from individual humans or from humans working in concert with one another. So you may prefer to believe that we each possess a divine spirit, but I see no evidence of that and, as an atheist, that is another one of the things I do not believe.

Some of you, I am sure, are attracted to the idea of a divine spirit in each of us because in your view, that is the part of us that survives after we die. In your view, if this life on earth is all that there is, then human existence is a big disappointment. As far as I am concerned, when our bodies die, our thoughts die (although they may survive us in books or objects or recordings) and that is that. There is nothing of us left except in the memories of others or in the works we participated in creating. I don't consider that view a bleak view at all. The only thing I think that believing in some sort of afterlife would add to my life would be to make my actual existence on earth a waiting game—like standing in line at the theater, waiting to get a glimpse of the "blockbuster" inside. That seems to make my life on earth appear *less* meaningful to me, not more so. Part of the reason that the things we do when we are alive are so important, is that there is nothing else. We find happiness, meaning, satisfaction, etc. during our lifetimes or not at all.

What about that sense of something bigger than ourselves, which many of us have? As I said earlier, when describing my personal religious/philosophical history, I too have often had a feeling that there was some intelligence besides my own with whom I shared my thoughts and to whom I could communicate. I came to realize that that sense of another being or another intelligence was produced by my own mind. It might have been a natural epiphenomenon from consciousness or it might have been created through my early teaching about a divine all-knowing presence, or perhaps by my internalization of the admonitions of my parents and other authority figures, or my collective sense of "others" (what George Herbert Mead called the "generalized other." Mead characterized thinking about oneself as the internalized dialogue between the "I"—myself as subject, and "me"—myself as an object to the others whose observations and judgments I have internalized).

I already mentioned that my own observation was that my past tendency to confide in some being inside of my mind appeared to me to be a variety of magical thinking, of the same kind that almost everyone engages in order to give them a sense of safety, or privilege, or to bring good luck. Just ask a baseball player, a gambler, or an NBA star about to shoot a foul shot, what his rituals mean to him. He may not say his is talking to god, but I'm pretty certain that he would say he feels as if he is addressing something greater than himself, something that will dictate the outcome of his baseball playing, his gambling or his foul shot. Repeating something that was accompanied by success, or by a reduction in anxiety in the past, even if that something is only a thought, might be adaptive to survival. A mechanism that caused an organism to automatically engage in such behaviors, even when the connection between the behaviors and the outcome was coincidental, might be useful. B.F. Skinner showed that rats, pigeons and dogs will engage in such "superstitious behavior." Both Daniel Dennett and Richard Dawkins provide suggestions as to how and why evolution may have favored such a tendency in us. Even if sometimes what is coincidental with success or with the avoidance of pain is actually not what caused that success or avoidance, it pays to have a mechanism built into us that leads us to repeat those behaviors without requiring us to know whether the causality is truly a fact.

Whatever it is that I sense as an entity to which I direct my thoughts, it belongs to my own consciousness, not to some entity outside of myself. Since in my case (I don't know about others) this sense of something seems to have a moralistic flavor—which I frankly find hard to separate from a fear-of-getting-found-out or a fear-of-getting-into-trouble flavor—I find that there are times when it pays to listen to it or even consult it to guide my behavior. Interestingly, recent research in psychology, neuroscience and animal behavior has strongly suggested that a moral sense may be built into humans' brains—and a precursor of it into the brains of other primates. Some research and theorizing (more of the latter than the former) has suggested that this inner voice (what Hermans has called the "dialogical self") arises from early parent-child interactions and Allan Schore has claimed that it plays a role in regulating not only our behavior, but our emotions. Hopefully, further research will show how this moral sense is manifested in terms of the kinds of neural networks required to support it and how these are modified by learning and experience.

Is God Really Necessary?

Chapter 7

Values

Aha! I hear you say. But if people are just flesh and bones and blood and there is no spiritual entity beyond each of us, how do we establish values? Since different cultures have different values, it seems obvious to me that cultural factors and learning of cultural traditions are involved in developing our value systems. Richard Haidt, in his book, *The Righteous Mind*, has suggested that there are six dimensions of moral values, each of these containing both poles of a particular value (e.g. care vs. harm or fairness vs. cheating) and these are built into all humans on an evolutionary basis and are recognized in all cultures. However, some cultures place more emphasis upon one dimension than on another. Well, as I said above, recent research in neuroscience, psychology and animal behavior has suggested that some attitudes, which we associate with values and morality, are indeed part of our genetic inheritance. These would be inclinations to feel and behave in ways that had improved the likelihood of our genes being passed on in the past. For instance, reciprocal behavior, in which we reciprocate if someone does us a good deed or in which we do a good deed for someone else in hopes of him reciprocating, are both likely to be inclinations that are built into us through our evolutionary history. Indeed, such behaviors are found in other species as well humans, from

27

chimpanzees to vampire bats. If we find that we have such behavioral or emotional inclinations we are also likely to construct an explanation for them, despite the fact that we are ignorant of their origins. So we produce the "golden rule," and in our minds it is our conscious adherence to this rule that produces our behavioral inclination. The opposite is in fact true— we constructed the rule because it puts into words an inclination that we found we had (which may be the reason that it is found in nearly all cultures and religions)—but once we publicly subscribe to the rule, then that will probably also increase our chance of acting in accordance to that rule (remember cognitive dissonance?). So we have a value and a verbal description of it and it is primarily due to our genetic history and the role language plays in controlling our behavior that the value has an effect on how we act. Which values we subscribe to and how strongly we endorse them is probably due to our cultural and individual learning histories.

For some people, their religious beliefs and the religious environment to which they have been exposed and in which they live, will, along with other factors in their culture, affect their values. Or so they believe. Richard Dawkins has presented an entertaining, but intelligent, rebuttal to this belief in his book, *The God Delusion*. Essentially, Dawkins shows that if people actually followed the moral precepts of the Bible, they would be considered immoral by the standards accepted by most of the present-day world. Remember, god asked Abraham to kill his son and Abraham (the "father" of Judaism, Islam and Christianity, but also of some real children), acquiesced (saved at the last minute from committing murder by god's change of heart). This was the same Abraham who, to save his own life, passed his wife off as his sister and lent her to the Pharaoh to use within his harem. Of course god punished the Pharaoh for falling for this charade, but Abraham got off Scott-free. This was the same god who saved Noah and his family while killing all other humans and all but two of every species of animal because god was angry. He also ordered Moses to tell his people to stone a man to death because he was gathering firewood on the Sabbath. But then Moses himself, also a revered figure in three major religions, instructed his priests to kill the thousands who worshipped the golden calf and ordered the slaughter of all the Midianites except for the virgin women, whom he told his soldiers to use for their own pleasure.

Now most people will respond to these accusations of bloodthirstiness in the values portrayed in the Bible with a claim that these are symbolic messages, not to be taken literally as prescriptions for how to behave in modern times. But what in the world could they symbolize other than murder, revenge and genocide? And if one can pick and choose which values to follow from the Bible and which not, then where does the moral sense which allows one to make such choices come from? Not from the Bible itself or that would be circular reasoning. The truth seems to be that our moral sense comes not from religion but from outside of it.

Some of you, who don't identify with Judaism, Islam or Christianity will tell me that my focus upon these three religions is too narrow. What about Buddhism, for instance? Isn't that an inherently peaceful religion, which uses meditation to see through the violent emotions that would otherwise overwhelm human beings? Of course it is, but then Southeast Asia, which has seen as much or more conflict over the years as any other place on the planet, is filled with countries that are overwhelmingly Buddhist. Eighty-five percent of the Vietnamese combatants on both sides of the Vietnam conflict were Buddhists (the Viet Cong and North Vietnamese, were officially atheists, since they were communists, but the atheism of Ho Chi Minh was not shared by most of the Viet Cong, or even the ordinary North Vietnamese soldier or citizen). In Thailand, there are armed Buddhist militia tasked with protecting Buddhist shrines and citizens. In Myanmar, Buddhist mobs, led by religious leaders, one of whom has referred to himself as the "Buddhist Bin Laden," have been responsible for countless Muslim deaths. Buddhist monks have claimed that their anti-Muslim campaign is mandated by the teachings of their faith and have named it the "969" movement, to symbolize the nine attributes of Buddha, the six qualities of his teachings and the nine attributes of the monks. The Sentinel Project for Genocide Prevention has labeled the 969 Buddhist movement in Myanmar a form of "ethnic cleansing."

Is God Really Necessary?

In Sri Lanka, Buddhists are at the forefront of mob attacks on the Muslim minority and monks accompany soldiers when they go on campaigns. While Chinese persecution of Buddhists in Tibet has gained headlines, it must be remembered that Buddhist mobs led by monks rampaged through the streets and burned the houses and businesses of Chinese merchants as a protest against China. And as has been amply documented, the Dalai Lama's palace in Tibet has torture chambers in its basement gruesome enough to rival those used by Saddam Hussein.

What about Hindus? Isn't *ahimsa* a principle of nonviolence that guided Gandhi and is part of both Buddhism and Hinduism? Doesn't it involve a recognition of the divine spirit that inhabits all living creatures? Certainly it does, but that hasn't kept Indian Hindus from attacking Indian Muslims on numerous, bloody occasions, such as the much-publicized killing of over a thousand Muslims during riots in the state of Gujarat in 2002, and of course, India, a primarily Hindu country, has armed itself with nuclear weapons.

Religion certainly aims to be a source of values, but in some cases, the values that appear to characterize the texts and teachings of our religions seem to be barbaric by modern moral standards. In other cases, the values sound wonderful, but they clearly fail to become internalized by the followers of the religion. And of course there are just the plain old illogical and nonsensical applications of religious values, which are much more prevalent than one would think (e.g. using the commandment, "Thou shalt not kill" to put a murderer to death, waging war in the name of someone who said to "love thine enemies").

It appears to me that values have changed over the centuries and that, in many, if not most cases, we have progressed to, in the words of George H. Bush, a "kinder, gentler" stance on many moral issues. And in most cases, this appears to be in spite of, not because of religion. The United Nations *Universal Declaration of Human Rights*, passed in 1948 affirms racial and gender equality, religious freedom and freedom from arbitrary or inhumane arrest and punishment. Subsequent international agreements have outlawed torture, genocide, discrimination on the basis of gender or race and forced child labor. Nearly 150 countries have outlawed the death penalty (the U.S. not included) and most recently, 16 countries have officially sanctioned same-sex marriages (which I regard as progress in values, although some people do not). Preserving our planetary environment has become a value for an increasing number of people worldwide, most recently probably as much out of fear of impending environmental disasters as out of a heightened awareness of the value of all living and non-living things on our planet, but this too is progress. Of course stating a value and living by it are two different things, as the history of religion has taught us, but in terms of values to which people subscribe or to which they aspire, I think the human race has made progress.

So people have values, those values have changed over time and still vary across cultures. Some are inspired by religion, but most are not and there is no logical reason why someone without a religion or sense of spirituality would not have values or even why his or her values would be much different from those of others within the culture in which he or she lives. So my values are pretty much the same as many other people in my culture. After all, the reason I am writing this book is because I am aware of that, but many people who share my values seem to think that I could not share theirs if I am truly an atheist. That is simply not true. My own values include the following (the list is a sample and is not exhaustive):

One human should not take another human's life.

Conflicts should be resolved without resorting to violence.

Wars are not a reasonable way to solve international or domestic disputes.

Everyone has the right to believe and express whatever opinion he or she wants to hold or express so long as it does not harm someone else.

All humans should be treated as equally valuable and given equal rights, regardless of race, sex, sexual orientation,

Is God Really Necessary?

intelligence, ability or disability, wealth, nationality, religion, or any other way of characterizing them.

All living things, including non-human species, are valuable and have rights to life and freedom.

Our planet's environment should be protected to as great an extent as is possible.

It is wrong for one segment of the population to have more resources than they need while another segment does not have enough resources to live without extreme discomfort.

It is the responsibility of all of us to insure that no one lives in such poverty or fear as to do them harm.

Children, being especially vulnerable and unable to defend themselves, need special protection from harmful things, such as ill health, poverty, lack of education, enforced labor, sexual predation, physical abuse, etc.

I don't think that any of the above values are at all unusual in my culture and, as I said before, I assume that I developed these values via the same mechanisms of cultural transmission as most other people did. Additionally, I hope that some of them represent natural inclinations of human beings, based upon our evolutionary heritage, although, frankly, the evidence for this is meager. Yes, doing unto others as you would have them do unto you, sacrificing oneself for the safety of others and care for those smaller or more vulnerable, as well as care for those who are related to us, can all be demonstrated in other species and are no doubt built into our genes in some form. But the modal behavior of millennia of human beings would argue against most of the values listed above being dominant human tendencies. That is why I also believe that it is necessary for me to actively promote these values in hopes of them becoming more prevalent in the behavior of myself and my peers, not just in our words.

Values may also be a product of reasoning, but the influence of reason on our values (or any other aspect of our behavior) should not be overestimated. Numerous studies in cognitive psychology (which happens to be my field), have demonstrated that it is quite unusual for people to make decisions based upon logical reasoning. Instead, we act based upon habits, upon reasoning from analogy ("this seemed to work in a similar situation, maybe it will work here"), upon influences of which we are only dimly or not at all cognizant. In addition, the preferences of our group can influence us with us only being aware of wanting to remain a valued part of the group. We feel that we have independently and logically formed our own decisions, but we have formed then in order to insure our continued membership in the group (a component of "group think").

We are the most logical and reasonable when we explain our behavior to someone else (or sometimes to ourselves), after the fact. And often we behaved the way we did not because of the logical reasons we give to explain our behavior, but for emotional, illogical or unknown reasons. But that is not to say that reasoning *can't* play a role in our decision making. People who try to persuade us of something don't just play upon our emotions and prejudices, they also try to present reasonable arguments. And sometimes these arguments work. This is true even in the arena of values. After reading Jonathan Haidt's well reasoned and well documented book, *The Righteous Mind*, for instance, I was at least open to understanding (but not adopting) some value systems I had previously rejected as completely misguided and incompatible with my own values.

Chapter 8

Guilt

What about guilt? If I don't believe in god or a higher power, then why would I feel guilty about doing anything? As an atheist, shouldn't I have an "I can do whatever I want so long as my fellow human beings don't punish me," attitude? I mean, if there is no god to punish me, then what have I to fear?

The truth is, it's very easy for me to worry about whether I have done or am doing the right thing. I often have the feeling that I've forgotten to do something very important, or that something I've done will turn out to have been misguided and will bring negative consequences. The feeling is not distinguishable for what we call a "nagging sense of guilt." I worry about such things much more than it turns out that I should, since I don't really do that many bad or even wrong things, at least in my own opinion. But worry and anxiety are not necessarily rational emotions.

I can turn even small activities into moral issues. Running the water too long while I shave or brush my teeth leads to guilt over wasting precious water in drought-ridden California. I am almost obsessive about not littering and about recycling waste. Driving a car that uses too much gasoline is a constant source of guilt for me (now that I drive a Prius, I feel a little

37

better!). Eating fast foods, drinking too much alcohol, taking a day off from my exercise routine, all of these are accompanied by nagging guilt, sufficient to make them only occasional lapses, but not sufficient to wipe them from by behavioral repertoire altogether. There have even been times when I have felt a queasy feeling in my stomach, something akin to dread, which told me that there was something I should be worrying about, perhaps something that I had done wrong, although I didn't know what. I would begin casting about for the source of this feeling, trying to find the incident or activity that I was worrying about or feeling guilty about. Then it turned out that the queasy feeling was the beginning of the flu, or a mild stomach upset, or part of a hangover.

As an atheist, I'm sure that I feel guilty about a lot of the same things that non-atheists feel guilty about. My guess is that this reflects several things: First of all, I have the kind of nervous system in which anxiety is easily aroused (but luckily for me, subsides fairly rapidly. Some people whose anxiety is easily aroused but does not subside quickly, develop such elaborate behaviors to avoid anxiety or reduce their anxiety that they are handicapped by them). Second, I was raised by parents (actually my mother much more than my father) who used guilt as a method of controlling my behavior. It was nearly impossible for me to have a good time without my mother bringing up something I should feel guilty about. When I went to a school dance in junior or senior high school, my date being the prettiest girl at the dance, my mother routinely asked me as soon as I arrived home, whether I had danced with the "wallflowers" who must have been "crushed" to go to the dance and not be asked to dance, especially by the popular boys such as myself. I dutifully *had* asked the wallflowers to dance, much to the chagrin of my girlfriend, but my mother always regarded my claim of having done so with skepticism. When I became a psychologist, working with severely disabled youngsters in a state hospital but also having a private practice and making a good enough income, between the two jobs, to buy a house, I told my mother about my good fortune. She told me that she was disappointed that I had become so interested in money that I put it before the welfare of the people I was supposed to be helping. Finally, the well-educated, middle-class, liberal social milieu in which I was raised and continue to live, tends to come up with a lot of things to feel guilty about (eating processed food, drinking carbonated beverages, consuming genetically modified grains, drinking alcohol, enjoying NASCAR, watching "commercial" television—the list is unending).

I was also exposed to religion. As I said in the beginning of this book, my exposure was inconsistent and a little out of the mainstream, but I did attend Sunday School and church where I was explicitly taught what was right and wrong from the point of view of my religion. The Christian Science religion may be one of the least guilt-provoking of any Christian religions. Nevertheless, at a young age, when I was religious, I sometimes imagined god watching me, even reading my mind, and holding me accountable for all of the things I did or thought. Most of what I did or thought did not violate any of the Ten Commandments, so what god ended up clicking his tongue at me about was the same set of things that my society and my parents clicked their tongues at me about. In fact, my parents one-upped god by overtly punishing me. When god dropped out of the picture for me, nothing really changed. I wish I could say that I lost my exaggerated sense of guilt, but I didn't.

Is God Really Necessary?

Chapter 9

Sacred and Interconnected

Both religious people and people who regard themselves as "spiritual," whether or not they are religious, have a tendency to invoke the concept of the "sacred." I have to admit that this usually turns me off, since as often as not, what they believe is sacred is something valued by them but not by me. I looked up *sacred* in the dictionary and found several definitions. About three-fourths of them related to something being *holy*, that is, connected to a god or religion. In terms of this aspect of the definition of sacred, there is nothing that fits that category for me. But I certainly recognize that there are things that are sacred to other people, such as the Bible or the Koran, religious dances or artifacts, mandalas, or crosses. I try to respect other people's views of what is sacred to them, so long as they do not violate others of my values (e.g. putting someone to death for destroying a sacred text, violates my value about killing human beings). But *sacred* can also refer to something highly valued or important or something deserving of reverence or respect. I do find that there are a host of things which fall into this category of sacred for me: great works of art, music or literature, the words and deeds of some great people, the Declaration of Independence.

Is God Really Necessary?

A meaning of *sacred* that I did not find in the dictionary, but which I believe is part of the connotation of the word, is that it is a *feeling* one has when experiencing something that may be regarded as sacred. By this I mean something akin to awe, the sense of the profound. Sacred music, especially choir music, may bring out this feeling in me. Some architecture, especially churches and mosques (but also Egyptian and Mayan pyramids), evokes such a feeling in me, as do a number of natural phenomena, such as the Grand Canyon, pictures of the earth from space, glaciers, and the ocean while standing on its shore. I think this feeling of strong emotion provoked by something that one considers sacred, is part of what some people refer to as a "spiritual" feeling. Well, I get these feelings too, without any ideation related to spirituality. But perhaps I am just not recognizing my own spirituality. Perhaps; but that is not what I think. I think that these kinds of feelings are built into human beings on a genetic basis, either because they brought some evolutionary advantage, or equally likely, that they were a by-product of some other adaptation that brought an evolutionary advantage (although I remember reading a study that purported to show that humans felt a sense of peace and security when they were located in a place that offered a wide vista around them and that such a feeling was hypothesized to be conducive to them residing in easily defensible positions, thus giving an evolutionary advantage to people who had the genes that produced this feeling).

Is God Really Necessary?

Closely connected to the feeling of some things being sacred, is the feeling that all things are interconnected. Many people, including myself, believe that all living things (and for me, even non-living things, such as mountains and clouds and oceans, water and ice) are interconnected. This is a central idea within many people's spiritual beliefs and is a guiding principle in their concern for the environment, for non-human species, and for humanity as a whole, instead of just the people who resemble them or whom they know. The interconnectedness of things is also a guiding principle in my concerns for all of the same things. The difference is that I think that such interconnectedness is a function of the way the material world works and has been demonstrated by many scientific findings. While spiritual people may regard such interconnectedness as a manifestation of an all-pervasive consciousness or spirit, which either inhabits or creates all of the reality around us, they are usually eager to cite the same scientific research which I cite, which shows that interconnectedness is a fact related to the laws that govern our world. For instance a consequence of war is to devastate the environment while at the same time an effect of environmental destruction, such as would be caused by global warming, is to increase the likelihood of war. Droughts in one location on our planet will influence weather, perhaps even causing floods somewhere else. Pollution from coal or oil burning power plants in one part of the world will affect global warming for all of us, while a decline in the bee population will cause a decline in our ability to produce food from plant life, and so on. Well, to my way of thinking, if science has demonstrated the connectedness of everything (and isn't that the main principle of ecology?) then why would I need to invoke spirituality to justify my belief in it? A spiritual belief may make the idea of interconnectedness feel more profound, or sacred or do I dare say, *sexy*, but these spiritual ideas are frosting on the cake. They are not necessary in order to believe in interconnectedness.

Chapter 10

Conclusion

I have tried to explain why I am an atheist and what that means about how I think about some important issues. I have not tried to argue against religion or spirituality, not tried to show that my non-belief is superior to others' belief. I do not claim to speak for any other atheists, nor do I know how typical my thinking on this subject is. I have read a very small number of books on atheism and some of my thinking, mostly in terms of comparing atheism to religious belief, has been influenced by such books. But most of the way I think about things is derived from a wide array of influences, probably more of them representing religious or spiritual people than atheists, simply because atheists are in a minority among the people with whom I interact. In many cases, I no longer remember where an idea came from or how I arrived at it. And as I have pointed out, the rationale for my conclusions about many issues is, in many cases, an explanation I have formulated in an effort to explain myself to others and the real reason I favor an opinion may be unknown to me.

I don't know if the world would be a better place if it was filled with a greater number of atheists, although I do believe that organized religion has been a source of many of the evil things done by man. But atheism has not had an opportunity to be the dominant belief of any large group and who knows what kind of havoc that could cause? There is no reason that I can think of that being an atheist would be linked to any other particular value, either a positive or negative one, so there is no reason to believe that all the motivations that govern human relations when the majority are religious would be any different if they were atheists. Right now, most atheists probably are people who have faith in science and believe in evolution, since these ideas are the source of many peoples' atheism. However, if atheism became the dominant attitude, then, like any other dominant attitude, most of the people who agreed with it would probably be people who did so out of conformity, without necessarily giving much thought to the reasons why they had such an attitude.

As I said in the opening chapter of this little book, my aim in writing it has been to show those people who share many of my values that an atheist can be more like them than they might think and that their spirituality or their belief in god is not a precondition for developing such a value system.

I hope that I have been successful.

Is God Really Necessary?

APPENDIX A

Consciousness and Reality

Quite a few people believe that there is scientific evidence that reality is created by consciousness. The experimental evidence most often cited in this regard is in the field of quantum physics and is evidence which demonstrates the effects of measurement on the outcome of the so-called, "double slit" experiment and its variations. Without going into the details of these experiments, the gist is that the pattern of photons projected one at a time through double slits onto a surface is one that is compatible with a wave form of the photon, while the same photon projected through a single slit produces a pattern compatible with a particle. However, measurement of the photon passing through the double slit alters the pattern so that it again appears to be a particle rather than a wave. The experiment itself is regarded as demonstrating that photons possess the qualities of both particles and waves. It also demonstrates the intuitively paradoxical finding that measurement, or observation, can alter the apparent behavior of a photon by fixing it in particle form (by identifying its location). These results, which are compatible with quantum theory and were predicted by Richard Feynman, have been the subject of intense scientific debate about their meaning. The accepted meaning for decades, referred as the "Copenhagen interpretation," was that stable reality, as we experience it everyday, is dependent upon someone observing it. This had led to theories of reality being "created" by "consciousness." Further research using this experimental paradigm and mathematical models however, have suggested that any interaction with the waveform of light, not necessarily involving a human consciousness, will "collapse" the waveform back into a particle in a process referred to as "decoherence." Other research on what is referred to as "entanglement" has demonstrated that when two separated quantum particles are aligned, they take on a seemingly inexplicable ability to respond to each other instantaneously, apparently violating Einstein's claim that nothing can travel faster than the speed of light. This finding, primarily because it seems to violate the theory of relativity, has been taken to mean that a) reality is constructed by the observers and need not conform to what is seemingly possible in a real world; b) the consciousness which supports this reality is simultaneously everywhere.

Quantum physics has had a counterintuitive flavor since its initial development. While some of its predictions are still unconfirmed, others have led to experimental confirmation. One of its basic principles has been that measurement or observation has an influence upon experimental findings. This has not been seen as an artifact (i.e. some form of experimenter bias), but as a characteristic of the reality described by quantum theory. This has led to a great deal of speculation about not only the role of the observer but about the characteristics of the observer as well as about the distinction between the observer and what is being observed. There is no consensus on these issues at this point. It is even fair to say that there is no agreement so far as the larger question of what descriptions of particle behavior at this subatomic level have to do with the reality with which we interact on a day to day basis (what cosmologist Max Tegmark calls our "consensual reality"). In fact, specifying the relationship between these two domains might be seen as the main task of modern physics.

Is consciousness part of the submicroscopic world of quantum mechanics or is it part of our consensual reality? Despite some notable efforts, there has been no convincing explanation of consciousness in terms of quantum mechanics. On the other hand, there is considerable agreement on the consensual characteristics of consciousness, although not in terms of physical variables. At this point, pending some theoretical or experimental breakthrough in biology, chemistry or physics, to specify the relationship between consciousness and physical variables remains the "hard problem," to use the words of philosopher David Chalmers.

Every neuroscientist will say that the world we perceive is a world shaped by the architecture and processes of our cognitive systems, which in turn have been shaped by evolution. We experience the world in the way which was most likely to lead to survival and procreation in our species' history, and it is not necessarily the same world that is "out there," in the ordinary language sense of external reality. This is easily demonstrated by showing that our minds are susceptible to illusions because of the built-in perceptual mechanisms we all possess. Most of these mental mechanisms are not ones of which we are consciously aware. We do not have conscious access to how we process visual stimuli to recognize faces, or how we process strings of sounds to recognize language. Our consciousness does not shape these processes, but they shape the contents of our consciousness. In some cases, scientists have been able to localize where, in the brain, such processes are being carried out and by which neural networks. They have also been able to document the loss of such processing abilities as a result of damage or disease. In such cases, the contents of consciousness are dramatically changed (e.g. a person is unable to recognize faces, sometimes even his own, or to understand language or to think in language). These findings and clinical demonstrations are important in defining the nature of consciousness. The view of consciousness which emerges from such findings is not one that is fully understood, but three things are certain: consciousness has evolved over the history of the development of the human race; it has evolved through interactions with external reality, and it is dependent upon the activity of the brain. These are facts which have to be taken into account in any description of the relationship between consciousness and reality.

Is God Really Necessary?

We have meager evidence of the influence of consciousness on the behavior of subatomic particles, evidence that is actually related specifically to measurement or observation, and only to consciousness by inference and extension. On the other hand, we have voluminous evidence that alterations in the brain can affect consciousness in lawful ways, whether these alterations are structural or chemical. In these cases, the consciousness that is altered by these physical changes is the familiar one of sensation, perception, cognition, and emotion. Given this state of affairs, to fasten upon the meager and controversial and quite possibly irrelevant data from quantum experiments and to ignore the substantial, replicated and theoretically clear data from neuroscience research, which leads to a view of consciousness being dependent upon, rather than causing physical states, seems chancy, at best. To theorize further about "universal consciousness," or a "vast potential" of consciousness, or a "force from which all of reality is created," seems premature, goes well beyond any extant data, and is purely speculative. To go even further and describe characteristics of such a consciousness as "expressing the relatedness of all things," or "demonstrating that love is the basis of all of reality," or to invoke the idea that human consciousness is part of some greater spiritual consciousness which transcends any particular human, can best be described as creative fiction.

Is God Really Necessary?

APPENDIX B

Is Consciousness a Physical Process?

Consciousness is not something separate from the neural networks which process information. The operation of these networks is what consciousness *is*. Now neurons differ from one another in shape and size, but they all function similarly. They release a variety of neurotransmitters and which ones they release can be important in emotions and in affecting the coherence of thoughts, including such subjective experiences as being able to separate thoughts from external perceptions (as in hallucinations), being able to disengage from a pattern of thinking (as in obsessions) or even the felt experience of being a separate being from one's environment (which can be affected by hallucinogenic substances such as LSD, which appears to affect neurotransmitter receptors). But the basic sense of being conscious of a sensation or experience or a thought seems to consist of a feedback system, which provides a simultaneous (or so it seems) "observer" experience of what a network is processing.

The neuroscientist, Walter J. Freeman, on the basis of a body of evidence from animal studies, has hypothesized that the brain stores information as meanings. These meanings are wave patterns of cortical activity that transition in discrete phases to represent the significance of stimuli (the stimuli's

52

association with positive and negative rewards, or with distinctive context, etc.). This kind of meaning includes both the representations of "outside" stimuli and the motivational activation related to our goals and intentions involving such stimuli. This information comes from our limbic system, so it also includes our memories of both the stimuli and their previous relationships to these goals. In other words, the stimuli to which we respond are represented within our brains in terms of their relationship to our goals and emotions (hunger, sex, achievement, danger, escape, fear, satisfaction, and in humans, in higher level verbal and socially mediated meanings). To say it another way, they are represented as meanings, not just as raw sensory stimuli. This is the way our brains work. We process the world in terms of its meanings and the interaction between these wave patterns of meanings produces consciousness, i.e. awareness of ourselves and the world in terms of meanings. Thus, in this system, consciousness is exactly an interaction going on between neural networks within the brain.

How such interactions work or of what they consist is a matter for physiologists to determine. Freeman, on the basis of his EEG studies, thinks that they involve very rapid wave changes across broad areas of the brain. Others, such as Fodor and Tegmark, see them as intricate feedback networks, confined to those areas of the brain which are dedicated to making information conscious.

Is God Really Necessary?

To the extent that conscious experience is a function of the type of network, rather than of the raw materials from which the network is constructed (in the case of the brain, it is neurons and their chemical composition), then consciousness could be achieved by non-humans, such as computers or robots which contained similar networks. This is only a theory, since it is always possible that consciousness is not just a property of such processing networks, but also of what the networks are made (e.g. the chemicals which are involved in neural functioning).

Is God Really Necessary?

APPENDIX C

Possibility and Impossibility

Someone (I forget who) has said that if we can imagine something, then its opposite cannot be a necessary condition for the world to exist. In other words, whatever we can imagine could have been a possibility. By this interpretation, it is simply a contingent fact that that particular something which we imagined is not true or does not exist. An extension of this (or perhaps an alternative interpretation of the same idea) might be that if we can create a mathematical structure, then it is possible for that structure to exist. This is part of the basis for doing theoretical physics at a purely mathematical level. But this formulation leads to a lot of confusion.

The confusion comes from trying to reconcile the "possible" with the world in which we live. We live in a world of particularities. These particularities include a fairly narrow range of physical variables (what has been sometimes referred to as the "fine tuning" of our universe), which are those that allow life as we know it to exist. In my example in the text of the sun standing still in the sky, which entailed the earth stopping its rotation, with nothing on earth affected, it is possible to provide a mathematical structure in which our forward-directed perception of time is nullified to the point that time "stands still," as in fact Einstein did in his relativity theory. However, time standing still in the case of relativity theory means that an instance in which *nothing* changes, goes on forever (this would only be true from the point of view of someone inside this system, which would have to be traveling at the speed of light). This is entirely different from the sun standing still while everything on earth continues as usual. Yet we can imagine this latter possibility, which is, in fact, impossible. It is impossible because in order for our world, with our oceans, our skies, our forests, our deserts, our flora and our fauna and ourselves in it to exist, all the physical conditions that describe our universe have to fall within fairly narrow parameters. So the particularities which we experience as our world are, in many cases, not arbitrary so far as their ability to sustain the world we know is concerned. Therefore, we live in a world which allows only limited possibilities, more limited than those that we can imagine.

Is God Really Necessary?

Bibliography

Anderson, P. , Dickson, D. & Silverberg, R. (1972). *The Day the Sun Stood Still.* Edinburgh: Thomas Nelson.

Chalmers, D. (1996). *The Conscious Mind.* New York: Oxford University Press.

Dawkins, R. (2006). *The God Delusion.* London: Bantam.

Dennett, D. C. (2006). *Breaking the Spell: Religion as a Natural Phenomenon.* New York: Viking.

Feynman, R., Leighton, R.B. & Sands, M. (1963, 2006, 2010). *The Feynman Lecture on Physics: The New Millennium Edition.* New York: Basic Books

Fodor, J. (1982) *The Modularity of Mind: An Essay on Faculty Psychology.* Cambridge: Bradford Books/MIT Press.

Freeman, W. J. (2000). *Neurodynamics: An Exploration of Mesoscopic Brain Dynamics.* London: Springer-Verlag.

Freeman, W. J. (2004). How and Why Brains Create Meaning from Sensory Information. *Intl. Journal of Bifurcation and Chaos, 14,* 515-530.

Is God Really Necessary?

Haidt, J. (2012). *The Righteous Mind: Why Good People are Divided by Politics and Religion*. New York: Vintage.

Hermans, H.J. (1992). The Dialogical Self: Beyond Individualism and Rationalism. *American Psychologist, 47,* 23-33.

Mead, G.H. (1934). *Mind, Self, & Society*. Chicago: University of Chicago Press.

Miller, S. L. (1953). A Production of Amino Acids Under Possible Primitive Earth Conditions, *Science, 117,* 528-29.

Schore, A.N. (1994). *Affect Regulation and the Origin of the Self*. Hillsdale, N.J.:Lawrence Erlbaum.

Tegmark, M. (2014). Consciousness as a State of Matter. *New Scientist,* April 12, 28-31.

Tegmark, M. (2014). *Our Mathematical Universe: My Quest for the Ultimate Nature of Reality*. New York: Afred A. Knopf.

Is God Really Necessary?

About the Author

Casey Dorman is a former college professor and psychologist who has worked in both the public and private sectors. He is author of eight novels and a collection of poems and short stories. He is also the Editor-in-Chief of *Lost Coast Review*, a quarterly literary journal. He has two children and five grandchildren and he and his wife, Lai, live in Newport Beach, California.

www.ingramcontent.com/pod-product-compliance
Lightning Source LLC
Chambersburg PA
CBHW060710030426
42337CB00017B/2829